GUIDE

MW01114316

Stewardship
Nurturing
Generous Living

Betsy Schwarzentraub
General Board of Discipleship

STEWARDSHIP

Copyright © 2012 by Cokesbury

This book is printed on acid-free paper.

ISBN 978-1-426-73639-1

Some paragraph numbers for and language in the Book of Discipline *may have changed in the 2012 revision, which was published after these Guidelines were printed. We regret any inconvenience.*

MANUFACTURED IN THE UNITED STATES OF AMERICA

Contents

Called to a Ministry of Faithfulness and Vitality

Y ou are so important to the life of the Christian church! You have consented to join with other people of faith who, through the millennia, have sustained the church by extending God's love to others. You have been called and have committed your unique passions, gifts, and abilities to a position of leadership. This Guideline will help you understand the basic elements of that ministry within your own church and within The United Methodist Church.

Leadership in Vital Ministry

Each person is called to ministry by virtue of his or her baptism, and that ministry takes place in all aspects of daily life, both in and outside of the church. Your leadership role requires that you will be a faithful participant in the **mission of the church,** which is to partner with God to **make disciples of Jesus Christ for the transformation of the world.** You will not only engage in your area of ministry, but will also work to empower others to be in ministry as well. The vitality of your church, and the Church as a whole, depends upon the faith, abilities, and actions of all who work together for the glory of God.

Clearly then, as a pastoral leader or leader among the laity, your ministry is not just a "job," but a spiritual endeavor. You are a spiritual leader now, and others will look to you for spiritual leadership. What does this mean?

All persons who follow Jesus are called to grow spiritually through the practice of various Christian habits (or "means of grace") such as prayer, Bible study, private and corporate worship, acts of service, Christian conferencing, and so on. Jesus taught his disciples practices of spiritual growth and leadership that you will model as you guide others. As members of the congregation grow through the means of grace, they will assume their own role in ministry and help others in the same way. This is the cycle of disciple making.

The Church's Vision

While there is one mission—to make disciples of Jesus Christ—the portrait of a successful mission will differ from one congregation to the next. One of your roles is to listen deeply for the guidance and call of God in your own context. In your church, neighborhood, or greater community, what are the greatest needs? How is God calling your congregation to be in a ministry of service and witness where they are? What does vital ministry look like in the life of your congregation and its neighbors? What are the characteristics, traits, and actions that identify a person as a faithful disciple in your context? This portrait, or vision, is formed when you and the other leaders discern together how your gifts from God come together to fulfill the will of God.

Assessing Your Efforts

We are generally good at deciding what to do, but we sometimes skip the more important first question of what we want to accomplish. Knowing your task (the mission of disciple making) and knowing what results you want (the vision of your church) are the first two steps in a vital ministry. The third step is in knowing how you will assess or measure the results of what you do and who you are (and become) because of what you do. Those measures relate directly to mission and vision, and they are more than just numbers.

One of your leadership tasks will be to take a hard look, with your team, at all the things your ministry area does or plans to do. No doubt they are good and worthy activities; the question is, *"Do these activities and experiences lead people into a mature relationship with God and a life of deeper discipleship?"* That is the business of the church, and the church needs to do what only the church can do. You may need to eliminate or alter some of what you do if it does not measure up to the standard of faithful disciple making. It will be up to your ministry team to establish the specific standards against which you compare all that you do and hope to do. (This Guideline includes further help in establishing goals, strategies, and measures for this area of ministry.)

The Mission of The United Methodist Church

Each local church is unique, yet it is a part of a *connection*, a living organism of the body of Christ. Being a connectional Church means in part that all United Methodist churches are interrelated through the structure and organization of districts, conferences, and jurisdictions in the larger "family" of the denomination. *The Book of Discipline of The United Methodist Church* describes, among other things, the ministry of all United Methodist Christians, the essence of servant ministry and leadership, how to organize and accomplish that ministry, and how our connectional structure works (see especially ¶¶[126–138).

Our Church extends way beyond your doorstep; it is a global Church with both local and international presence. You are not alone. The resources of the entire denomination are intended to assist you in ministry. With this help and the partnership of God and one another, the mission continues. You are an integral part of God's church and God's plan!

(For help in addition to this Guideline and the *Book of Discipline*, see "Resources" at the end of your Guideline, www.umc.org, and the other websites listed on the inside back cover.)

Stewardship and Generosity

Joyful, faithful, Christian **stewardship** is our way of living with all that God has entrusted to us, sharing and using it on behalf of God. When we live as stewards of the gospel, we show the Good News by our actions in and out of church, in total life commitment to God, and in loving people and all of God's creation. Stewardship involves developing core life practices that change us personally and transform the culture and behavior of our congregations.

But for many people, *stewardship* carries too many overtones of fundraising without a real basis in our faith. Over the years, scores of preachers and church leaders have used it as a cover-up word for "Give us your money!" while they borrowed secular funding techniques out of context. So a recent trend has been to use *generosity* to express authentic, deep-reaching Christian stewardship rooted in the gospel, not in secular consumer culture.

At a certain point in our lives, we realize that all that we are and all we have comes from God. In this moment of gratitude, we recognize God as the most generous giver of all (see John 3:16) and seek to use more and more of ourselves to demonstrate God's love through Jesus Christ (1 Timothy 6:17-19).

Generosity is a matter of heart, intention, and action. Generous living is not just about giving money, or even just about giving. It has to do with the whole of who we are and how we care for our neighbors, beginning with God's generosity toward us. In grateful response to God's love, each of us uses our heart, mind, soul, and strength. The Hebrew word for *heart* is literally the *leaning* or *thrust* of our lives. Generous-hearted living involves 100 percent of our lives, not just what we give to others or our "religious" thoughts and actions.

So how do we act as stewardship leaders in our local church? By nurturing generosity in our own lives and in our life together as a congregation, personally modeling and intentionally growing generous faith as joyful, self-giving stewards. With your stewardship and generosity team explore the questions and read the Scripture texts in this Guideline. This will help you develop as a team and discern the particular work God has called your team to do.

---

1. To what degree do your church leaders and members practice whole-life discipleship, including good stewardship of body, mind, and soul?
2. In what ways do we teach and model generous hearts and actions, practicing stewardship and not just fundraising?

The Stewardship and Generosity Team

as stewardship leaders, your main function is **nurturing generous living** in everyone connected to your faith community. So how to begin? Strongly resist the idea that your sole task is to conduct an annual giving program. The role of the stewardship and generosity team does not arise out of the church's need for funds, but rather out of personal need, as Christians, to give back to God in every dimension of life. So your team responsibilities are wide in scope, and may include the following:

Create a plan to build a congregational culture of generous-hearted living, including strong stewardship education for all ages, reporting focused on changed lives, a ministry-centered budgeting process, and a connection to mission that identifies giving as an investment in God's work.

Encourage individuals to grow more vibrant and faithful as stewards of the gifts God has entrusted to them. These gifts include their time, abilities, money, assets, relationships, involvement, and advocacy for others (see 1 Corinthians 12:1-13). Helping them learn how to get out of debt and the grip of consumerism frees them to put God first in their daily lives.

Prompt the congregation to develop as a vital community of gospel stewards. This involves a small group network for learning, sharing and service, comprehensive stewardship education, care for the earth, and exploring the Wesleyan legacy of stewardship practice.

Provide a lens through which church members see their stewardship as discipleship-in-action in the full range of local church ministry. Explore United Methodist and other resources for children, youth, and adults. Collaborate with community leaders to put plans into action.

Plan and implement a program to increase personal financial commitment to God's work through the church. This involves making a personal connection with people and situations that can be transformed through giving and encouraging first fruits living as an essential part of Christian life.

Inspire and invite people to participate fully in the church's connectional covenant, including apportionment shared ministries. Tell stories year-round about where your giving makes a difference.

Offer channels through which people can support God's mission locally, regionally, and around the world. These channels may come through the church, ecumenical communities, or in response to world events.

Visually, you can see your team responsibilities this way:

Each part of this graphic describes a different aspect of the stewardship and generosity team and is explained further in this Guideline.

The primary way your team nurtures generous living is by **building a culture of generosity**, both as individuals ("vibrant, faithful stewards") and as a congregation ("the church as a vital community of stewards"). You build a generous culture from two different angles: by inviting members to make their financial commitment and to support the congregation's work, and by relating to the full ministry of the local church, not just to church finances.

All ministry is done within the context of seeing stewardship as support for the church's mission. The mission to which God has called us includes participating in the wider connection we have as United Methodists in shared ministry around the world.

1. To what degree do your church leaders connect stewardship with the non-money aspects of all that God has entrusted to you?
2. Where do you see aspects of comprehensive stewardship and generosity lived out in the life of the congregation?

Core Stewardship Practices

b old, joyful stewards are not born, but made. As people practice more generous behavior over a lifetime and learn more about God the generous giver, they realize that authentic giving starts with giving themselves first to God in Christ, and that this is abundant life.

Lifelong Financial Stewardship
2 Corinthians 8:1-7

Stewardship education needs to be a lifelong process. Using the resources listed in this Guideline, your stewardship and generosity team can plan a range of learning opportunities and experiences in classes and small groups, fostering a sense of personal connection in the shared ministry of Apportionment giving, in mission trips, and ministry-of-money experiences.

By designing these experiences into an intentional local church plan, you help children, youth, and adults confront the persistent consumer-oriented culture that surrounds us and would otherwise saturate our lives. Such events also help us challenge the resulting fundraising ethos within the church. Instead of acting as if the church were one more competing organization for limited funds, we teach generosity as giving *to* God *through* the church, not out of obligation or membership, but from **gratitude to God** for the Good News in our lives.

Growing lifelong stewards requires a plan for teaching stewardship and generosity to young children, in youthful years, and throughout our adult lives. The stewardship and generosity team has the honor of providing and implementing such a plan as an ongoing gift to the congregation. These offerings of opportunities must be repeated on a regular basis. Not everyone is ready to hear this information at the same time.

First Fruits Living—2 Chronicles 31:4-10

Many people, especially in North America, begin with optional consumer spending (those things that look so good at the moment on our televisions, computers, and all around us). Then they stretch to try to pay their bills: food and shelter; real needs as opposed to wants. Finally, they see if there is anything left over for the church, and of course there often isn't. In fact, they're usually financially upside down, swimming in debt!

By contrast, first fruits living is the practice of **giving to God the first and the best of what we have, and managing all the rest according to God's generosity**. This is the goal for how we're meant to live. It is true for money, but also for time and relationships. We can give the first of each day in devotions; the first of each week in worship; the first of relationships in some key Christian friendships; and the first of our income, whatever is the best percentage we can give at the time in order to manage *all* of God's money entrusted to us. So first fruits living is about earning and saving as well as giving—all three of these dimensions—to reflect God's priorities.

It's a huge shift in thinking and lifestyle and affects every part of our family life. It means *unlearning* false ideas we have been taught, such as that stewardship and generosity are just about money, or that the tithe (ten percent) is the magic number we are meant to give to God. So how does first fruits living square with tithing—giving ten percent of our income—which The United Methodist Church lifts up as the standard baseline for giving?

In the Scriptures, tithing is the floor, not the ceiling. It is a "means of grace" (meaning a way we experience God's grace in our lives), a way to honor God, reorder our priorities, and realize our dependence on God. Some people take a long time to grow up to giving a full ten percent, and others can go far beyond it. The issue is making God's work a priority and reordering our lifestyle to reflect *God's* generosity, to the degree that we can.

In Matthew 23:23, Jesus assumes tithing as a basic practice, but says the practice is supposed to point us to "the weightier matters of the law: justice and mercy and faith." In a way, first fruits living starts at the *other* end from percentage giving and even tithing. Instead of asking, "How much can I give?" it prompts us to ask, "How little can I live on in order to be extravagantly generous?" In 2 Corinthians 8:9 Paul puts it this way, "Though [Jesus] was rich, yet for [our] sakes he became poor, so that by his poverty [we] might become rich." So first fruits living is a way to acknowledge this huge gift from God, responding with trust and love.

1. What might first fruits living look like in your life? How might it change your priorities?
2. What would be different if your church leaders practiced first fruits living? Would apportionments and mission be the first things paid each month?

The Faithful Financial Steward
Luke 19:1-10

Part of your work as a team is to help people grow in their financial stewardship, not only from occasional to systematic giving, but also from annual giving to including major gifts and planned giving, as well.

Annual giving is part of our basic expression of faithfulness to God through the church. In addition to stewardship education, your team can assist the finance committee in creating good financial policies, budget development and communication, special offerings and projects. You can communicate the "why" of giving (God and the gospel) and connect giving with key results in people's lives. (See "Ways to Track Our Growth.")

Major giving requires us to rearrange our priorities in order to give above and beyond contributions for the usual work of the church. Your team can make the case for why the church is a good recipient for such efforts as new land or facilities, renovation or debt reduction, missional opportunities, or establishing or growing an endowment.

Growing stewards realize they want to leave a legacy to future generations through bequests and other planned gifts. Your team can embrace a long-term plan to encourage people to make enduring gifts to God's work. This effort is not a self-contained program, but ongoing communication backed by available resources for when the time is right in the context of the individual's life.

Growing Vibrant, Faithful Stewards

Vibrant, faithful stewards express their thankfulness to God in prayer, reflection, conversation, and worship. They learn and practice basic stewardship principles, sharing and managing well their time, abilities and resources.

Personal and Family Finances—Luke 6:37-38

Many people see themselves as living far away from the ideal of giving back in response to having received so much from God. They feel trapped by debt, no matter what their income level. The stewardship and generosity team can give them the resources to get their finances in order so they can lessen their anxiety, reduce their fears, and get out of debt; give first to God's work; and plan realistically for both the present and the future. Helping them get the skills and courage to make this shift may be the most significant gift of stewardship that your team can give the congregation.

It is important to choose one core course on family finances and offer it at least once, though preferably twice, each year. By making these courses available to the community, the course becomes an entry point into the church for new disciples and members.

Depending upon your church setting, theology, and learning style, you may choose *Freed-Up Financial Living* from Good $ense Ministry or Dave Ramsey's *Financial Peace University*. No matter which one you choose, make sure it speaks to your church and age group, helping them learn financial skills; identify key biblical principles; challenge the lure of consumerism; and put together an action plan for responsible sharing, saving, and spending (in that order).

Once individuals are able to come out from under the cloud of debt—or even have a debt reduction plan that they are actively pursuing—they can start connecting their gifts of time, energy, and money with a clear sense of God's mission. They can see giving as a key indicator of a spiritual relationship with God, and take further steps of giving to change lives: both others' and their own.

Growing Expressions of Faithfulness
Luke 12:32-34

The stewardship and generosity team has a wonderful opportunity to help people in the congregation develop into faithful and effective Christian stewards in their use of time, abilities, relationships, personal involvement, and advocacy for others—in other words, in their prayers, presence, gifts, service, and witness. It is a joy to "uplift one another" in the faith community! As a team, seek to trust God's abundant provision and to reframe conversations in the church from a focus on scarcity to a focus on using your assets, teaching and preaching Scripture from the viewpoint of God's generosity toward all.

Begin by casting a vision of people as stewards of time, energy, wisdom, and body, connected to one another and to God. Abandon a "one-size-fits-all" approach to involvement in the church and respond instead to how much people are involved at this specific time in their lives. This includes encouraging one another in accountability and openness to the gifts of the greater whole. Engage and critique your surrounding culture together as a community of faith.

As you delve further into God's generosity and your lives, as stewards of all God has given, foster a church climate that supports people dealing with the power of money in their lives. Seek to bring money under control as a tool for living instead of as master. Interpret mission and your common connectional giving, and share stories from your personal stewardship journeys. Ask, "How is God at work here? What is God providing for our work?"

Stewardship in Different Generations
Micah 6:8

We do not all start in the same place or perception, not only because of our individual perspectives, but also because of the generation in which we live.

Leadership in many of our churches is dominated by Baby Boomers (those born between 1946 and 1964) with the continued presence of the older Silent Generation (born between 1926 and 1945) and the Builders (the G.I. Generation, born before 1925). But what about Gen Xers (1965–1981) and Millennial Generations Y and their younger counterparts in Generation Z (1982–1992)? How do we engage these next generations in significant stewardship, modeling for them and learning from them about generous-hearted living?

The Millennial generations would heartily agree with Jesus when he tells the Pharisees that tithing is fine, but don't forget "the weightier matters" of justice, mercy, and faith. The Center for Philanthropy at Indiana University cites studies showing that people born since 1981 are 20 percent more likely to say they give to improve the world. They want to see tangible changes in people's lives, such as wells dug or sustainable food grown and distributed equitably, for long-term transformational change. Jesus' terms of justice, mercy, and faith come under this category and so does the world itself: balancing the needs of the earth and all creatures with the press of human demands.

For Generations X, Y, and Z, giving is most commonly seen as an investment and the beginning of a relationship. They want to be involved and interactive, and expect collaboration. They want to feel a personal connection with the cause and know what happens after they give time and money. What difference does their giving make?

The "generalized trust" that Baby Boomers and older folks tended to have toward the church and other institutions has worn away. Gen X and Millennials have replaced it with "strategic trust," which is based upon proven relationships with specific trustworthy individuals. So follow-through stories about the difference our giving makes are of paramount importance. Engaging people born anytime since 1964 must include **visible change, measurable growth, and audible feedback**, showing the relevance of their giving for long-term transformation. Their gifts of time and contribution to meaning are their great rewards.

The advent of social media is not just another trend; it has transformed communications and affects every part of our lives. Five hundred million people connect regularly through Facebook, 150 million use MySpace, and 35 million use LinkedIn. Twitter and Tumblr are the preferences of most Y and Z generations, bypassing email, with 18 million and 3 million users, both on the rise. We must **share stories electronically**, inviting people to be involved, and allowing them to give through a variety of electronic means, as well.

---

1. How does your church help people deal with debt and the devouring logic of consumerism?
2. In what ways can you intentionally invite Gen X and the Millennial generations to invest themselves in "the weightier matters" through the work of the church?

The Church as a Vital Community of Stewards

how can we help our church mature into a vital congregation where disciples are growing in their faith, engaged in and sharing their resources for mission? In other words, how can we help them grow into a community of dynamic gospel stewards? As you begin creating a plan to build a culture of generosity, gather guidance from our Wesleyan heritage and be reminded of our crucial role in caring for the earth.

John Wesley and Small Group Life
Acts 2:42-46

John Wesley's motto of "Earn all you can, save all you can, give all you can" offers a powerful framework for a simplified lifestyle that challenges acquiring at the expense of others and hoarding when others do not have the necessities for living. The books *Simple Rules for Money* and *Enough* (see the Resources section) can be excellent studies to unpack implications for how we can not only "do good" but also "do no harm" (John Wesley's phrases) in the complexity of economic life today.

But that's not all. John Wesley saw comprehensive stewardship as embedded in Christian discipleship; it is at the heart of the Wesleyan revival. In fact, one purpose of the small groups was to receive money for the shared ministries of the Methodist movement. This network of small groups helped people grow in their relationship with Jesus Christ through their use of time, prayer, abilities, and income that God had entrusted to them.

Small groups are the heart of the church alive today. In them, participants can deepen in their faith, be accountable in community, and do hands-on mission. The Simple Church movement emphasizes our need for this monumental shift from supporting the institution, as does the *Call to Action* of The United Methodist Church. We seek to "engage disciples in mission and outreach" with gifted, equipped, and empowered lay and clergy leadership. This can happen best in small groups that include children and youth and that are designed to encourage, support, and hold people accountable in their Christian walk.

We can hold stewardship discussions in Bible studies and new-member classes. We can offer legacy giving seminars, personal-finance training, and stewardship teaching in confirmation training and youth activities. A network of small groups for all ages helps people thrive in their faith, encourage one another to grow, and teach and practice generous living.

Care for the Earth—Psalm 104

The Bible is filled with Scriptures about God as our generous Creator and our call to care for the earth and all of God's creatures. In *Earth Trek: Celebrating and Sustaining God's Creation,* Joanne Moyer highlights the importance of our care for creation, including how:

- **God delights in Creation** and cares for the well-being of all creatures (Genesis 1).
- **Creation reveals God's character** (Romans 1:19-20). All creatures praise God (Psalm 19:1-6; Psalm 148). Wilderness places facilitate close encounters with God (Exodus 3:1-2).
- **Creation belongs to God** (Psalm 24:1). Everything the earth produces is God's gift. The earth supports life through God's grace, not human effort.
- **Human beings are part of God's creation and have a special role and responsibility within it** (Genesis 1:26; 2:15).
- **God's plan includes restoring Creation.** The earth will produce bountiful gifts (Amos 9:13), predators and prey will live in harmony (Isaiah 11:6-9), and the result will be a new heaven and a new earth (Revelation 21:1).
- **We have a moral relationship with Creation,** which is affected by our actions. God blesses our faithfulness by causing the earth to flourish (Deuteronomy 28:1-6) and uses natural forces to punish human sin (Jeremiah 14:1-10).
- **Jesus has a role in creating and restoring Creation.** He is the first-born of Creation and participates in creating the world (Colossians 1:15-16). He has authority over Creation (Luke 8:22-25), and its restoration is part of the salvation he brings.

The church can teach and practice care for the earth in countless ways, from stewardship education classes to offering community toxic clean-up days; from inviting environmental stewardship practices to challenging consumerism. The sky's the limit!

1. What can you do to create small-group settings where people can practice more deeply generous behavior?
2. How can you encourage one another to reduce your consumption? To distinguish wants from needs? To simplify your lifestyles and live below your means?

Building a Culture of Generosity in the Church

great ministry does not happen by chance; it requires an intentional plan. So it is with building a culture of generosity in the congregation, beginning with a strategic plan, drawn up by the stewardship and generosity team, and implemented in all areas of church life.

Essential Elements of a Plan
Luke 14:28-33

These three practices are essential to the plan.
1. Address comprehensive stewardship, not just finances or funding.
2. Have both long-term and short-range goals.
3. Lift up key church ministries visually in an interactive way, through an Annual Report or Scope of Ministries. Fill the experience with stories showing changed lives as a result of your generous involvement and support of God's work.

Using those essential practices or strategies, build a lively, holistic plan for strengthening generous behavior and attitudes. Include these components.

A statement of what you believe—This affirmation connects your mission with support of time, money, and involvement. It states your basic congregational understanding of the relationship between faith and money (for example, tithing and/or first fruits living).

Leadership—Look for staff and lay leaders who model generosity in their lives, with whatever gifts they have been given.

Stewardship education—Plan learning experiences for children, middle school, youth, and adults (see Resources section). Include aspects of both growing joyful individual stewards and congregations as steward communities. Include the connection between mission and how to give.

Communication—Design an ongoing way to tell people about the changes God is making through you. Keep it positive, personally-connected, and persuasive (moving from information to motivation). Create a process of "Ask, Thank, Tell" (see Resources section). Report to individuals quarterly on their financial giving.

Ministry-centered budgeting process—This includes doing a hard evaluation of fund-raising events. Are they more for raising money or for building community? Help people rely on their planned financial giving as much as possible (see Financial Commitment Programs section).

Annual financial commitment process—Only part of its purpose is funding programs. Help the finance committee communicate clear expectations, invite a step up in giving, and say thanks for the response.

One-on-one cultivation—Larger churches include individual visits by the pastor and/or generosity staff person for major donor development.

Capital giving—Include major gift programs as needed to expand ministries. They may be all-in-one or done by phases.

Planned giving—Make a case for why people should make planned gifts for God's work through the church. Focus on wills and bequests (the most common planned gifts) and include guardianship for young parents. Set up a local church endowment fund, policy, and spending plan. Start or strengthen a long-term plan to promote planned giving.

End-of-year giving—This is not an "annual lamentation"! Most churches receive 40 percent of their income in the last two months of the year. Report on what you have accomplished with the people's generosity, and list what could happen in the new year.

A plan is a working document that keeps you on track moving toward your goals. It is designed to be flexible as your lives unfold, so you will want to adjust it every quarter or every six months. Begin with the "Result" phrases in the section called "Ways to Track Our Growth" at the back of this Guideline. Pick up any ideas that fit your church from the sample strategies and methods there, and ponder the ten components above. For each component, start where you are and then think about what would be the next step. And be sure to help people celebrate victories as you go!

The Pastor's Role—Exodus 36:1-7

The pastor is not only a spiritual leader but a financial leader, as well. But this financial role can be difficult for many ministers to fill because of their own towering seminary debts, lack of financial and stewardship training, or fears that people will think they are just trying to raise their own salaries.

But God's reign addresses use of church funds as well as those of individuals and families, and people are yearning to hear an authentic message from their pastors about ministry and money. *Ministry and Money* (see the Resources section) is an outstanding contribution to pastors at any point in their vocation. It reminds us of the ways money can take over a congregation's life by being hidden, and describes a healthy theology of money and its relationship to discipling. It discusses church budgets, accounting and financial transparency, money issues in the pastor's life, and connecting money and mission.

When pastors step up alongside the stewardship and generosity team and the finance committee, they can help their congregations use money as a gift and tool for ministry instead of an object for coercion, selling, or begging. They can make sure the budget arises out of God's vision for the church. And they can invite people to first fruits living and the full range and depth of biblical stewardship in our everyday lives.

Financial Commitment Programs
2 Corinthians 9:6-10

Christian financial commitment programs are not commercial breaks in order to fund the congregation's ministry. They come straight out of the Good News as part of our ministry and emphasize the need of the giver to give, not the need of the church to receive. Their purpose is to emphasize growth in people's lives as disciples of Jesus Christ; encourage commitment to faith through first fruits living; teach and model extravagant generosity; and highlight financial responsibility as faithful, joyful stewards.

By rotating different types of financial commitment programs every few years, you appeal to people who have various ways of learning and involvement. This way, more people are drawn into leadership; you tie in the themes with different aspects of ministry; and the approaches stay fresh. See www.gbod.org/stewardship for a listing of programs by types. For example, "Common Hope, Common Trust" is a meal approach, and "Go and See" is a Stewardship Fair type. "I Have Called You Friends" is a small-group model, and "Special Delivery" is a home visit approach. "Extraordinary Generosity: The Heart of Giving" is an outstanding, substantive example of the Commitment Sunday approach.

Whatever specific program you choose, the Texas Methodist Foundation notes that you need to:

Create the vision—Describe the scope of your ministry, the distinctive elements (the church "DNA"), and the focus or emphasis for the coming year.

Gather information—Determine what church members need to make an informed decision about their support of the church's ministries. Decide who will gather this information, and through what channels (visual, verbal, social media) so it speaks to both head and heart.

Confirm your theological foundation—Choose what Scripture is your primary basis for this approach; what biblical story or theme; and your view on first fruits living, tithing, and proportionate giving.

Plan for implementation—Decide the ways you will help givers make a personal connection, the time period for your implementation phase, what you need to do to prepare, and questions you might anticipate to answer.

Mobilize resources—Discuss who will need to do what and when, how much it will cost and how it will be paid for, and what will be the system of accountability.

Communicate the vision—Convey inspiration, describe the difference it will make in people's lives, and make a powerful personal connection.

Prepare for celebration—Decide the date and logistics for Commitment Day, how you will inform and excite people about it, what follow-up you will have with those not present, and how you will bring a joyful completion to your efforts.

Remain thankful—Work out ways to acknowledge every commitment made to the church's projected ministries, review your record-keeping methods and revise them if needed. Keep the information flowing throughout the year about individual, family, and congregational support.

1. What is the first step you can make to create a plan to build a culture of generosity in your congregation?
2. How can you bring freshness, variety, and theological authenticity to your next financial commitment program?

Relate to the Congregation's Full Ministry

When the stewardship and generosity ministry is distinct (not linked solely to Finance), it can work with every aspect of our church's ministries.

Worship—Matthew 22:34-40

The work of the stewardship and generosity team can empower and "make real" our worship life as we witness daily to God's grace out of gratitude for God's abundant love. Conversations on critical issues of stewardship of life can begin in the pulpit and deepen in small group explorations. We naturally integrate stewardship into worship by doing four things.

Use stewardship-related resources, such as lectionary-based offertory prayers (www.gbod.org/stewardship), "Radical Gratitude"—stewardship reflections on lectionary texts (www.umfnw.org, in Stewardship Emphases), and connectional giving stories and bulletin inserts (www.umcgiving.com).

Preach stewardship almost every week. Nearly every Bible text refers to some aspect of stewardship and generous living. Practicing loving God with all your heart, soul, mind, and strength reflects God's generosity. Preach boldly about money (not just funding), including what the Good $ense Ministry names as the five financial aspects of Christian living: diligent earner; generous giver; wise saver; cautious debtor; and prudent consumer.

Nurture young stewards regularly, helping them to see, value, and offer the gift of who they are and what they have to God through their relationship with others. Start with the "Stewardship Nuggets" (children's sermon messages). See resources at www.gbod.org/stewardship.

Celebrate the offering as an act of worship. Use an offering invitation or story that connects people's lives with God's mission. Provide paper hearts for worshipers to make a personal response to the sermon invitation and put in the offering plate. Have slips of paper available for electronic givers to give at offering time. Write a "Now that's great stewardship!" statement for worshipers to read in the bulletin beneath the offertory line and on the worship screen. Have people come forward with symbols of the ways this community makes a living. Find more ideas in *Celebrating the Offering* (see Resources).

Christian Education—Deuteronomy 6:1-9

Lifelong stewardship education is a key part of Christian education: learning about God as the most generous Giver, God's initiating grace, and our lives as gifts to be shared according to God's priorities for the sake of all. The more we learn about God the Giver and God's creating, redeeming, and sustaining love, the more we seek to live in loving relationship with God and to reflect God's generosity in our living.

In the early church, Barnabas modeled generous living by selling his primary asset of land and giving the proceeds to support God's work through the church. He is an example of how generous giving can undergird and shape authentic discipling ministries (Acts 4:32-37).

Teaching generous-hearted living is an important part of Christian education. It needs to begin with young children and grow through teenage years, so that understanding and practicing generosity can grow as we mature. Adults need to keep testing out more trusting and modeling behavior as we deepen in our faith. We can use small groups, Sunday school, classes, retreats, Vacation Bible School, mission trips, special offerings, and church-community interface events to make this lifelong stewardship connection.

---

1. How can you strengthen the stewardship message within your church worship experiences?
2. When and how do you currently begin teaching about stewardship? How can you extend your efforts toward lifelong learning?

Lay Leadership—Luke 21:1-4

As you choose your church leaders, look for and encourage people who exhibit the following qualities:

1. **Training and perspective**—A comprehensive understanding of Christian stewardship, effective in cultivating financial stewardship, motivational and clear in communications, and psychologically healthy in regard to money
2. **Skills**—Ability to speak to groups, manage time and resources, organize for a task, build and motivate a team, and listen to values and goals
3. **Enthusiasm about your church**
4. **Positive commitment** to God through your ministries
5. **Sets a good example of generous giving** of time, talents, spiritual gifts, finances, care for the earth, and planned giving
6. **Practices first fruits living, tithing, and proportionate giving**

Growing leaders who possess these qualities help raise the level of vision for the church; encourage people to give of themselves, not just their money; invite an atmosphere of freedom for people to share about their giving; and challenge others to join in generous living.

Participating in Shared Ministries

When we become members of the body of Christ in The United Methodist Church, we join both a local church and a worldwide network of person-to-person ministries. We become part of a connectional covenant that spans the globe, positioned to transform the lives of individuals and communities through intersecting relationships and resources as God at work in the world.

A Worldwide Network—Acts 1:8

"Apportionments" are intentionally given from one local community to another through the network of the church. Just as a magnetic field transfers energy, church agencies work through the World Service Fund and other global and conference channels to bring help to those most in need.

Part of the role as the stewardship and generosity team is to interpret, promote, and advocate full support of your congregation's apportioned giving, and to help one another understand the importance of connectional giving—not as a tax or to shore up the denomination, but as a mandate of the gospel to care for those whom Jesus loves. Together, we can do what no one individual or congregation can do alone. We do this with accountability and joy, measuring and celebrating the difference our shared giving makes.

When we give money through our churchwide connection, it helps develop principled Christian leaders for the church and the world. It builds new churches to bring people to Christ, and it teaches lay and clergy leaders how to revitalize existing congregations. We engage directly in ministry with people both nearby and geographically beyond our reach. As a team, you can share stories of need and of lives changed because of the generosity of those who have given to God through shared United Methodist ministries. Use ideas from the "Daily Strategy for Pastors" (www.umcgiving.com).

Communicate personal stories. Speak about where apportionments touched someone's life and made a difference. Tell stories that come from a variety of settings: global, regional, and local. Some people are passionate about one situation and not another. If you only show one side of mission, you will not reach the whole congregation.

Invite retired pastors in the church to help raise apportionments. They help members see how apportionments support those who have faithfully served the church. They also can show how various local ministries form a network of compassion and advocacy throughout the annual conference.

Use Sunday bulletins, newsletters, photos, DVDs, video presentations, and websites to tell heartwarming stories. Positive stories of people aided by United Methodists foster a good sense of belonging to The United Methodist Church. Sharing stories that touch people's lives and demonstrate godly generosity can motivate your congregation to give to God through the apportionments.

Remind members that apportionments are not an administrative cost or a tax, but ministry. Draw a connection between being in ministry and finding ways for people to experience their gifts in action. Supporting a homeless ministry, for instance, may seem daunting at first, but it can revolutionize ministry as people see how their gifts change lives.

Make a Personal Connection
2 Corinthians 3:2-3

People do not give to budgets or causes or even ministries, but to people. We all need to know good things are happening because of our giving, and the best way to know this is by seeing it firsthand. When someone who gives to or receives from a specific ministry can speak to us in person, by Skype or DVD, they become more than a number or a need. They create a personal connection. Even an email or a letter with a picture can help your congregation imagine the life of that teacher, missionary, intern, or church worker. Someone in a nearby congregation or a colleague in your conference may have a personal relationship with a person or group who are positively affected by denominational generosity and can help the ministry "come alive."

People connect with one another through communities, shared practices, ways of thinking, and common involvements. All of these linkages help us realize how close we are to one another. As a local church team, emphasize projects that excite your members and with which they can identify.

The point of these stories often is "God is always faithful" or "God is merciful and just" or "We are in this together" or "You can do it too." Like Jesus' parables, stories of God at work through your giving allows you to recognize what your hearts already know.

How can you help your church members experience an exciting personal connection with the persons and ministries you support through your giving?

Stewardship for Mission

inviting Christians to share who they are and what they have with others is asking them to put their resources at God's disposal. This deep generosity is at the heart of community with other Christians and all who receive from their giving.

Communicate the Vision—Matthew 28:18-20

Communicating God's vision for your work is not a ploy to get money out of people. It is a way to remind them of God's self-giving for the sake of the world and that every inch of our lives comes from that grace. It also calls the congregation into deeper commitment to the particular ministry to which your church has been called. So giving is receiving is giving, in a continuous cycle of grace.

Generous, joyful stewards keep practicing what it means to be a disciple of Jesus. Steward leaders encourage others to keep growing in this process whenever they send timely thank-you's to all who give gifts, tell givers what they are helping to accomplish, and invite opportunities for deeper involvement. Two-way communication is important between givers and church leaders, to explore common values and engage personally in community through small groups or classes, ministry, ecumenical gatherings, and more.

In a world of fragmentation and distraction, help church members keep their focus on mission.
1. Be bold when you talk about money, following Jesus' example.
2. Always put giving of oneself and one's possessions in the context of gratitude and discipleship.
3. Talk about our own experiences.
4. Model a growing edge of giving.
5. Preach, teach, and practice tithing and first fruits living.
6. Be creative and use humor.
7. Work for the long haul.

Giving for Future Generations—Psalm 89:1-2

Through planned giving, we give to God's future ministries through the church to help children yet unborn experience God's presence and hear the Good News. "Planned giving" usually is created by an estate planning professional and may be distributed either now or in the future. It comes from assets, not income, and is given in addition to regular, ongoing support of the church. Often the fact of having given a planned gift increases our personal commitment to the church's present ministries, as well.

But the sad fact is that an estimated 70 percent of all people do not have a will or revocable living trust when they die. Without a will, state laws follow a formula that leaves nothing to the church or any other charity. Churches that rely solely on income gifts experience increasing competition for tight current funds and limit their future ministries.

The most common planned gift is a will or revocable living trust, but a wide array of specific financial vehicles exists to fit unique situations. The United Methodist Foundation in each annual conference can suggest the best options for individual circumstances. To contact your Foundation, call your Conference office or go to www.naumf.org.

Preparing an estate plan is good Christian stewardship—thanking God, expressing our love and concern for family, and showing charity toward others. We share our faith beyond our lifetime and have the joy of knowing that whatever we do not use in this life will continue in ministry after our death.

Planned giving has nothing to do with the size of your church or the size of the gift. It is not only for the rich, either. In fact for most people, a planned gift will be the largest financial gift of their lifetime. Planned giving provides a way to witness to deep values and high priorities, whether they are expressed through the local church or wider ministry connection.

Encouraging planned giving in the congregation says that you believe in the future of your church; that you want to build a sense of permanence in what you do. Planned giving by members of the congregation models good stewardship as a church family, above the expectation of each person as a good steward. Offer members the opportunity to examine their Christian stewardship in a broader context, to learn about many planned gift opportunities for mission and ministry through the church, and to leave a legacy of faith to future generations.

1. How do you relate great stewardship to the vision God has for us in the world?
2. Do you have an ongoing strategy in your congregation for promoting planned giving? How can you encourage awareness of planned giving opportunities?

Ways to Track Growth

Once you have employed the suggestions for nurturing personal and congregational stewardship, how do you know if you have achieved the results you want? If stewardship were only about money, it would be easy; you could count how many people are giving, whose giving is up or down, and how much they have contributed. But stewardship is about having a fruitful and generous *life* in all aspects, and that may be harder to measure.

The chart on page 29 provides a visual way to identify what you are doing (or plan to do) and what effect it has on your congregation. First, determine and define the results you desire, such as:
1. Growing vibrant, faithful stewards (personal growth)
2. Maturing as a vital congregation of gospel stewards (congregational growth)
3. Building a local church culture of generous hearts and lives
4. Strengthening the stewardship of the church's full ministry
5. Empowering our worldwide mission connection.

Second, there is a flow of ministry for any congregation, and stewardship can be emphasized in some way in each area of activity. This flow is described in the *Book of Discipline* (¶122), and can be summarized as 1) **reaching** out to receive people, 2) **nurturing** new disciples, 3) **equipping** disciples for ministry, and 4) **sending** out disciples of Jesus Christ into the world. Using a sampling of those expected results and the four ministry emphases in the discipleship flow, you may define your results and establish strategies for them, such as these.

Result 1: Growing Vibrant, Faithful Stewards. Members of the congregation are grounded in the biblical foundation of stewardship and take responsibility for their own first fruits living.

Strategies:
- Hold a stewardship-focused continuing education event annually (reach)
- Provide small group opportunities for teens and for adults to explore money and values (nurture)
- Offer annual Good $ense classes on *Freed-up From Debt* or other money management resource (equip)
- Sponsor a mission event that features local, district, conference, and global ministries (send)

Result 2: Maturing as a Congregation of Gospel Stewards. Members of the congregation embrace and advocate for a church-wide culture of generosity and stewardship, including how individual members and the congregation care for Creation.

Strategies:
- Hold a stewardship ministry fair, such as *Go and See*, available from the Ecumenical Stewardship Center (reach)
- Establish a separate stewardship and generosity team to create and implement a plan to cultivate a congregational culture of generosity (nurture)
- Set up and implement a process of spiritual gifts discovery for youth and adults (equip)
- Conduct community interviews to identify area constituencies, their needs and concerns (for stewardship of service and witness) (send).

Result 4: Strengthen the Stewardship of the Church's Full Ministry. The leaders of the church recognize the interconnectedness of stewardship throughout all ministry areas and work together to promote first fruits living systemically.

Strategies:
- Establish a system such as *Ask, Thank, Tell* to acknowledge and thank givers regularly (reach)
- Practice creative ways to express the offering time in worship, involving children and youth (nurture)
- Work with the lay leadership committee to recruit leaders who model good stewardship (equip)
- Have the stewardship and generosity team members talk about the stewardship aspects of each ministry area with its leaders (send)

From these strategies, the next step is to define how you will know if you have achieved what you want. Terms you may be hearing in your church are *measures* or *metrics*. For purposes here, *measures* would be the things you can count, such as increased giving or the number of people who participate in the groups or studies you have conducted. *Metrics* refer to the qualitative results; that is, what you can observe or your members report about their own sense of growth toward first fruits living. The stories people tell about the changes in their lives are a more compelling measure and witness than numbers in your record books.

The chart on the next page is a sample of what your metrics and measures might be for **Result 1: Growing Vibrant, Faithful stewards**.

SAMPLE: Measures and Metrics for Result 1—Growing Vibrant, Faithful Stewards

It may seem daunting to write out strategies and measures for multiple goals. The point is to begin to match your intentions with your results and to evaluate thoughtfully what you are actually accomplishing. Start with whatever you can and build on it until you have a sufficient portrait of the transformation your stewardship efforts are producing.

Definition:			
Members of the congregation are grounded in the biblical foundation of stewardship and take responsibility for their own first fruits living.			
Strategy 1: Stewardship focused continuing education event	**Strategy 2:** Small groups for teens and adults to explore money and values	**Strategy 3:** Offer annual "Free from Debt" classes.	**Strategy 4:** Sponsor mission event
Measures and Metrics (How do we know?)			
1A. 10% of the church's active adults attend the class	**2A.** 40% of active college-bound seniors attend a group	**3A.** 10% of congregation attends a class	**4A.** 10% of church attendees go on a mission team
1B. 40% of attendees report understanding the concepts of gratitude, first fruits living, and abundance thinking	**2B.** 30% of attendees change at least one of their consumer habits	**3B.** 30% of attendees initiate or revise their personal budget	**4B.** 30% of congregation supports the team with money, prayers, and/or supplies
1C. Six months later, 25% of attendees give to God the first of each pay period	**2C.** 30% of attendees begin pledging or increase giving to God's work	**3C.** 20% of attendees reduce their debt	**4C.** 10% of church responds to team's stories by giving time or money to mission recipient group

Resources

**indicates our top picks

BIBLICAL STEWARDSHIP AND YOUR ROLE IN THE CHURCH

Afire with God: Becoming Spirited Stewards, by Betsy Schwarzentraub (Nashville: Discipleship Resources, 2007. ISBN 978-0-88177-520-4).

**The Attributes of a Biblically Generous Church*, by Michael Reeves, at www.christianstewardshipnetwork.com/white_papers.php.

**Five Practices: Extravagant Generosity*, by Bishop Robert Schnase (Nashville, Abingdon Press, 2008. ISBN 978-1-426-70005-7).

Let the Children Give: Time, Talents, Love, and Money, by Delia Halverson (Nashville: Discipleship Resources, 2007. ISBN 978-0-88177-501-3).

Radical Gratitude (stewardship reflections on the Three-Year Lectionary texts) at http://rg.nwumf.org.

Stewardship in African-American Churches: A New Paradigm, by Melvin Amerson (Nashville: Discipleship Resources, 2006. ISBN 978-0-88177-452-8).

Stewardship Ministry Team Leader job description, www.gbod.org/stewardship.

FINANCIAL STEWARDSHIP IN THE CHURCH

**Ask, Thank, Tell: Improving Stewardship Ministry in Your Congregation*, by Charles R. Lane (Minneapolis: Augsburg Fortress, 2006. ISBN 978-0-8066-5263-4).

Creative Giving: Understanding Planned Giving and Endowments in Church, by M. Reeves, R. Fairly, and S. Coon (Nashville: Discipleship Resources, 2005. ISBN 978-0-88177-470-2).

**Extravagant Generosity: The Heart of Giving Planning Kit*, by Michael Reeves, Bishop Robert Schnase, and Jennifer Tyler (Nashville, Abingdon Press, 2011. UPC 843504019143); includes Daily Readings, Program Guide, Small Group Leader Guide, Timeline and Worship resources.

Faith and Money: Understanding Annual Giving in the Church, by Michael D. Reeves and Jennifer Tyler (Nashville: Discipleship Resources, 2003. ISBN 978-0-88177-410-8).

Giving: Growing Joyful Stewards in Your Congregation (Ecumenical Center for Stewardship, published annually), www.stewardshipresources.com.

**Ministry and Money: A Practical Guide for Pastors*, by Janet T. and Philip D. Jamieson (Louisville: Westminster/John Knox Press, 2009. ISBN: 978-0-66423-1989).

The Whys and Hows of Money Leadership: A Handbook for Congregational Leaders Just Getting Started, by Mark L. Vincent, www.designgroupinternational.com.

GIFTEDNESS AND GIVING
***29 Gifts: How a Month of Giving Can Change Your Life*, by Cami Walker (Cambridge: Da Capo Press, 2009. ISBN 978-0-7382-1356-9).

Celebrating the Offering, by Melvin and James Amerson (Nashville: Discipleship Resources, 2008. ISBN 978-0-88177-526-6).

***Equipped for Every Good Work: Building a Gifts-Based Church*, by Dan R. Dick and Barbara A. Dick (Eugene: Wipf and Stock, 2011. ISBN 978-1-61097-240-6).

LIFESTYLE AND STEWARDSHIP OF MONEY AND POSSESSIONS
Earth Trek: Celebrating and Sustaining God's Creation, by Joanne Moyer (Scottsdale: Herald Press, 2004. ISBN: 13: 978-0-8361-9291-9). 1-800-759-4447.

***Enough: Discovering Joy Through Simplicity and Generosity*, by Adam Hamilton: Book (Nashville: Abingdon Press, 2009. ISBN 978-1-426-70233-4), Stewardship Program Guide (ISBN 978-1-426-70287-7) and DVD.

Financial Peace University Home Study Kit, by Dave Ramsey (ISBN: 9781934629307IND). Includes Book; Financial Peace University Workbook; Audio CD Library; Budgeting Forms; two FPU CD-Roms; FPU Envelope System; Tip Cards; and Debit Card Holders. www.daveramsey.com.

**Freed-Up Financial Living*, Good $ense core curriculum, by Dick Towner and John Tofilon: Participant's Workbook (ISBN 978-074419637-5) and DVD, at www.goodsenseministry.com.

Freed-Up From Debt: How to Get Out and Stay Out, by Matt Bell, Participant's Guide (ISBN 978-0744198577) and DVD, at www .goodsenseministry.com.

Freed-Up in Later Life: Planning Now for Beyond 65, by Dick Towner, Participant's Guide (ISBN 978-074419858-4) and DVD, at www .goodsenseministry.com.

Money Sanity Solutions: Linking Money + Meaning, by Nathan Dungan (Minneapolis, 2010. ISBN 978-0-578-06998-2) www.sharesavespend.com.

The Power of Enough: Finding Contentment by Putting Stuff in Its Place, by Lynn A. Miller (Scottsdale: Herald Press, 2004. ISBN 978-1-893270-022-0).

WESLEY AND GIVING
Sermon 50, "The Use of Money," The Works of John Wesley: Volume 2.

**Simple Rules for Money: John Wesley on Earning, Saving & Giving*, by James A. Harnish (Nashville, Abingdon Press, 2009. ISBN 978-0-687-46616-0).

"A Wesleyan Perspective on Christian Stewardship," by Bishop Kenneth L. Carder, www.bwcumc.org/content/components-wesleyan-stewardship.

WEBSITES
Ecumenical Stewardship Center: www.stewardshipresources.org

Faith and Money Network: www.faithandmoneynetwork.org

**General Board of Discipleship: www.gbod.org/stewardship

Good $ense Ministry: www.goodsenseministry.com

National Association of United Methodist Foundations: www.naumf.org

Sharing God's Gifts—United Methodist Communications: www.umcgiving.org

Vital Congregations planning helps; see especially "Measures Evaluation Tool" in the "Setting Goals" tab. www.umvitalcongregations.com